Relax. Color. Learn Cursive.

Welcome to *The Art of Cursive*, the only adult coloring book that allows you to learn cursive and improve your handwriting almost effortlessly while you relax and color. CursiveLogic® is a patent-pending method that has been used by thousands of children and adults to master cursive handwriting. The lessons in *The Art of Cursive* are abbreviated lessons intended for adults. **To learn more about our comprehensive program for children, visit www.cursivelogic.com.**

The CursiveLogic® method has two unique features. First, rather than teach letters alphabetically, CursiveLogic® groups letters based on the shape of the initial stroke. Every lowercase letter in the cursive alphabet begins with one of four basic shapes. All similarly-shaped letters are taught together as a group. Second, all the letters in a group are taught as a connected string, allowing you to internalize the flow of cursive from the very beginning.

In the pages that follow, you will find four short lessons that teach all 26 lowercase letters. Each lesson first asks you to practice the basic shape that is common to all the letters in the group. Next, you'll find a letter string to trace, link, and write. When tracing, linking, and writing the letter strings, begin at the small arrow (▲). Do not lift your pen until you have completed the entire string. Each shape string has a short "Catch Phrase" to repeat as you form each letter. The phrase describes verbally the motion you are completing manually. Repeating the Catch Phrase helps to build muscle memory. Use the chart at the end of the lowercase lessons to review or learn the uppercase letters.

Once you have completed the lessons, it is time to start coloring! To best enjoy each image, carefully remove the page from the book at the spine. The pages are designed to easily pull away from the binding. Removing each page will allow you to easily rotate the page as you complete the various cursive shapes and words that make up the image. Start by using the back of the page to practice writing the quotation. To maximize your cursive practice, try filling in the elements with single strokes rather than the small coloring motions often used in adult coloring.

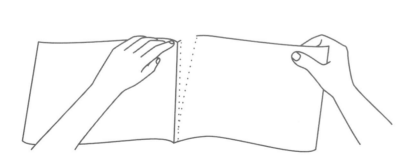

REMOVE THE PAGE FROM THE BOOK AT THE SPINE

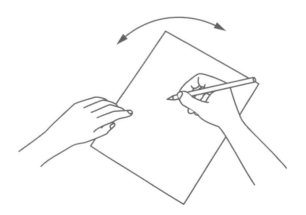

ROTATE THE PAGE AS YOU COMPLETE
THE VARIOUS CURSIVE SHAPES

Orange Ovals: Form the First Stroke

Start here (▲). Say, "OVER, BACK-TRACE."

Start on the baseline start point (▲).

Say, "**OVER.**" Pause, then back-trace around the oval shape to the baseline saying, "**BACK-TRACE.**"

TRACE

TRACE

WRITE

Cursive **LOGIC**

Trace the Letter String

Start here (▲). Say, "OVER , BACK-TRACE [LETTER NAME] . . . DIP."

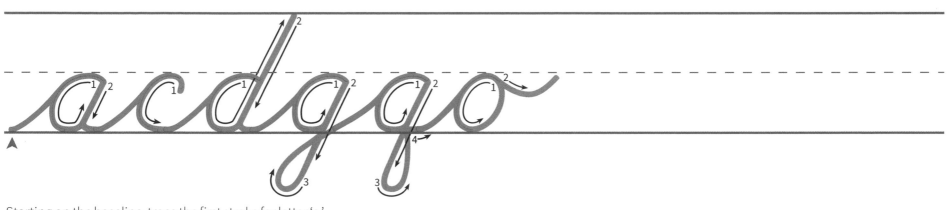

Starting on the baseline, trace the first stroke for letter 'a.'

Say, **"OVER."** Pause, then back-trace and complete 'a' saying, **"BACK-TRACE [a]."**

Each time the pen touches the baseline at the end of a letter, repeat the process for the next letter without lifting the pen. For the final stroke of 'o' make a small curve under the midline and say, **"DIP."**

TRACE

acdggo   *acdggo*   *acdggo*   *acdggo*

Add the first stroke to link the letters as you trace the complete letter string.

LINK

acdggo   *acdggo*   *acdggo*   *acdggo*

WRITE

Cursive **LOGIC**

Lime Loops: Form the First Stroke

Start here (▲). Say, "LOOP LEFT, DOWNSTROKE."

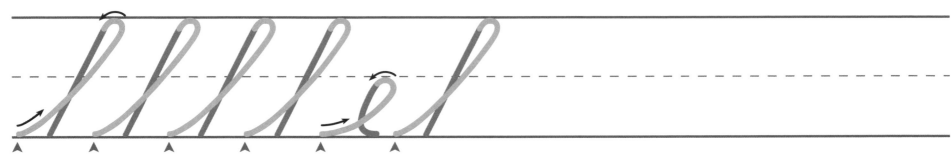

Start on the baseline start point (▲).

Say, "LOOP LEFT." As you reach the gray, say, "DOWNSTROKE."

TRACE

TRACE

WRITE

Cursive**LOGIC**

Trace the Letter String

Start here (▲). Say, "LOOP LEFT, DOWNSTROKE [LETTER NAME] . . . DIP."

fhkleb

Starting on the baseline, trace the first stroke for letter 'f.'

Saying, **"LOOP LEFT."** Pause, then downstroke and complete 'f' saying, **"DOWNSTROKE [f]."**

Each time the pen touches the baseline at the end of a letter, repeat the process for the next letter without lifting the pen. For the final stroke of 'b' make a small curve on the midline and say, **"DIP."**

TRACE

fhkleb   *fhkleb*   *fhkleb*   *fhkleb*

Add the first stroke to link the letters as you trace the complete letter string.

LINK

fhklib   *fhklib*   *fhklib*   *fhklib*

WRITE

Cursive **LOGIC**

Silver Swings: Form the First Stroke

Start here (▲). Say, "SWING RIGHT."

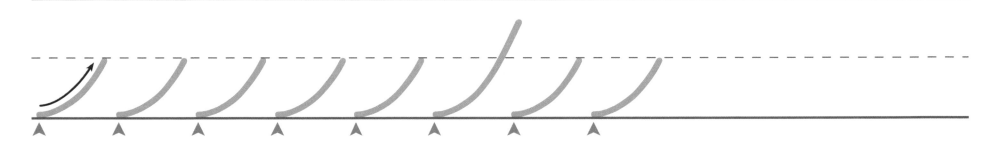

Start on the baseline start point (▲).

Say, **"SWING RIGHT."**

TRACE

TRACE

WRITE

Cursive**LOGIC**

Trace the Letter String

Start here (▲). Say, "SWING RIGHT [LETTER NAME] . . . DIP."

Starting on the baseline, trace the first stroke for letter 'i.'

Say, **"SWING RIGHT."** Pause, then downstroke and complete 'i' saying, **"[i]."**

Each time the pen touches the baseline at the end of a letter, repeat the process for the next letter without lifting the pen. For the final stroke of 'w' make a small curve on the midline and say, **"DIP."** Dot 'i,' dot 'j' and cross 't.'

TRACE

ijprstuw   *ijprstuw*   *ijprstuw*   *ijprstuw*

Add the first stroke to link the letters as you trace the complete letter string.

LINK

ijprstuw   *ijprstuw*   *ijprstuw*   *ijprstuw*

WRITE

Cursive **LOGIC**

Mauve Mounds: Form the First Stroke

Start here (▲). Say, "MOUND ROUND, DOWNSTROKE."

Start on the baseline start point (▲).

Say, **"MOUND ROUND."**

TRACE

TRACE

WRITE

Cursive **LOGIC**

Trace the Letter String

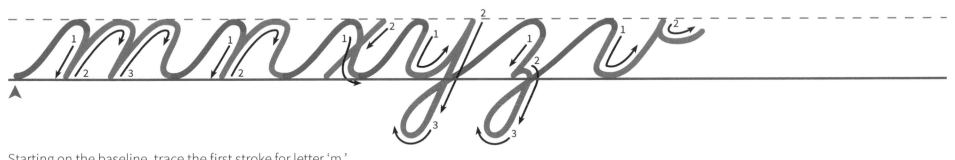

Starting on the baseline, trace the first stroke for letter 'm.'

Say, **"MOUND ROUND."** Pause, then downstroke and complete 'm' saying, **"[m]."**

Each time the pen touches the baseline at the end of a letter, repeat the process for the next letter without lifting the pen*. For the final stroke of 'v' make a small curve on the midline and say, **"DIP."**

TRACE

Add the first stroke to link the letters as you trace the complete letter string.

LINK

WRITE

*EXCEPTION: You may lift the pencil and cross 'x' while saying 'x.'

www.cursivelogic.com

Uppercase Letter Reference

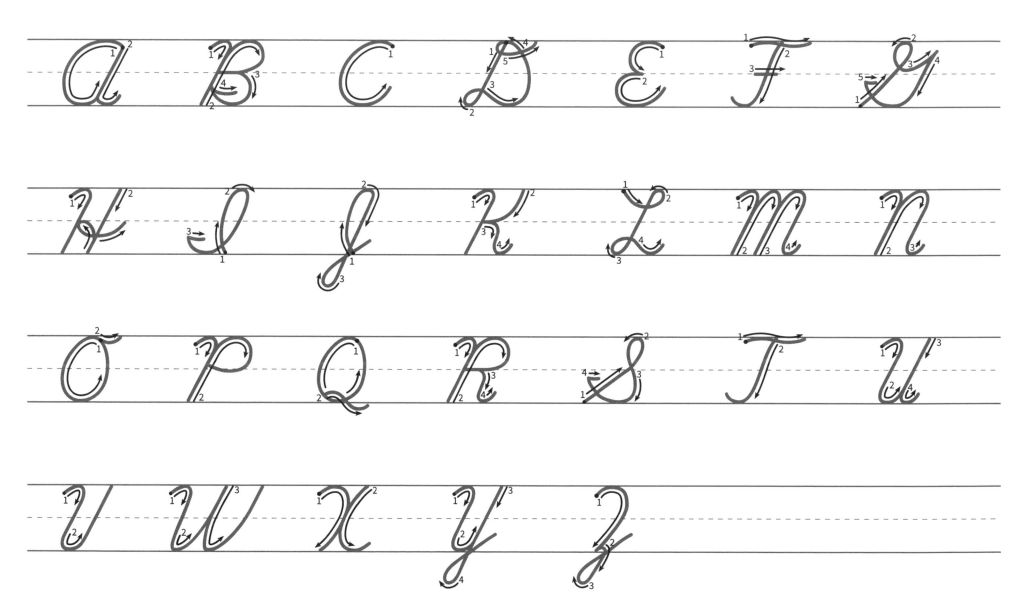

CursiveLOGIC

Be like the bird, who halting in his flight
on limb too slight
Feels it give way beneath him,
yet sings
knowing
he hath wings.

"Be Like the Bird" by Victor Hugo

Practice

Be like the bird, who; Halting in his flight,

On limb too slight, Feels it give way beneath him,

Yet sings; Knowing he hath wings.

"Be Like the Bird" by Victor Hugo

For my part I know nothing with any certainty, but the sight of the stars makes me dream

— Vincent Van Gogh

Practice

For my part I know nothing with any

certainty, but the sight of the stars

makes me dream.

— Vincent Van Gogh

But I,
being poor,

have only my dreams,

dreams
under your feet,

I have spread

my

Tread softly

because

you

tread on
my dreams.

"The Cloths of Heaven"

by William B. Yeats

Practice

But I, being poor, have only my dreams;

I have spread my dreams under your feet;

Tread softly because you tread on my dreams.

"The Cloths of Heaven" by W. B. Yeats

The wind and the waves are always on the side of the ablest navigator.

—Edward Gibbon

Practice

The wind and the waves are always on the side of the ablest navigator.

— Edward Gibbon

Practice

He is like a tree planted by water, that sends out its roots

by the stream, and does not fear when heat comes, for

its leaves remain green, and is not anxious in the year

of drought, for it does not cease to bear fruit.

WRITE

Build for yourself a strong box,

Fashion each part with care,

When it's strong as your hand can make it,

Put all your troubles there.

"Then Laugh" by Bertha Adams Backus

Practice

Build for yourself a strong box, Fashion each part

with care; When it's strong as your hand can

make it, Put all your troubles there.

"Then Laugh" by Bertha Adams Backus

I bequeath myself to the dirt

Complete the sentence in cursive

"Leaves of Grass"
by Walt Whitman

Practice

I bequeath myself to the dirt

to grow from the grass I love.

"Leaves of Grass" by Walt Whitman

"The Old Astronomer to His Pupil"

Though my soul may set in darkness, it will rise in perfect light;

I have loved the stars too fondly to be fearful of the night.

by Sarah Williams

Practice

Though my soul may set in darkness, it will

rise in perfect light; I have loved the stars too

fondly to be fearful of the night.

"The Old Astronomer to his Pupil" by Sarah Williams

Practice

All nature sings and round me rings

the music of the spheres.

— Maltbie D. Babcock

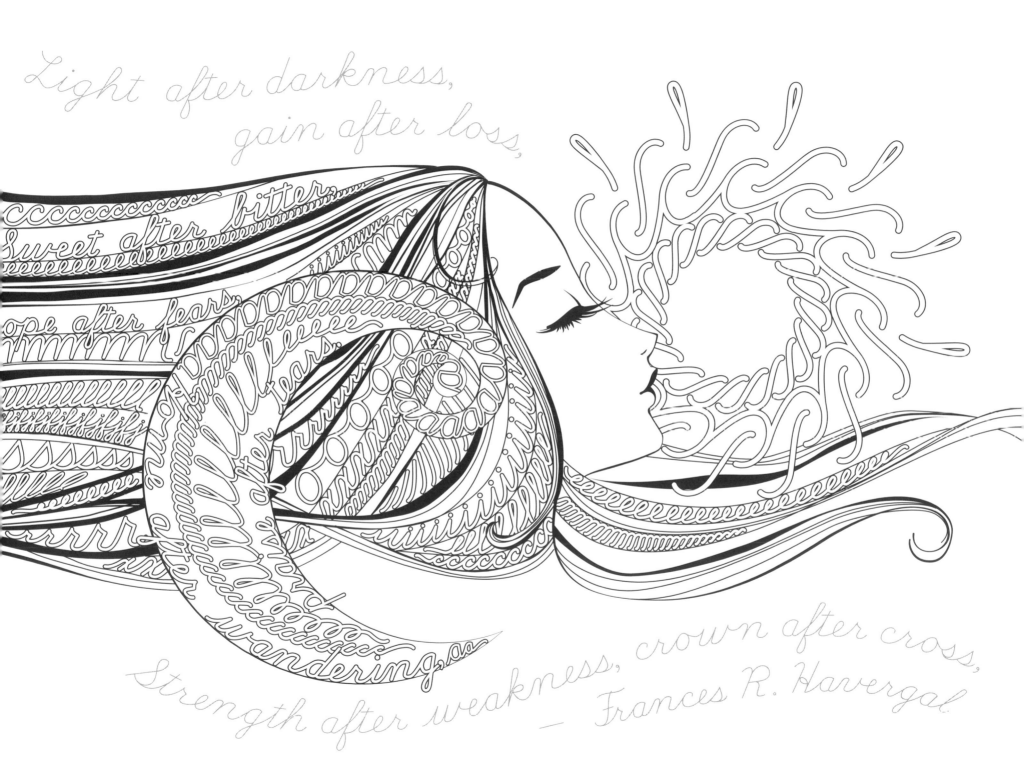

Light after darkness,
gain after loss,
sweet after bitter,
hope after fears,
Strength after weakness, crown after cross,
— Frances R. Havergal

Practice

Light after darkness, gain after loss, Strength after

weakness, crown after cross; Sweet after bitter, hope

after fears, Home after wandering, praise after tears.

- Frances R. Havergal

The star of the unconquered will,

He rises in my breast,

Serene, and resolute, and still,

And calm, and self-possessed.

— Henry Wadsworth Longfellow

Practice

The star of the unconquered will, He rises in my breast, Serene, and resolute, and still, And calm, and self-possessed.

— Henry Wadsworth Longfellow

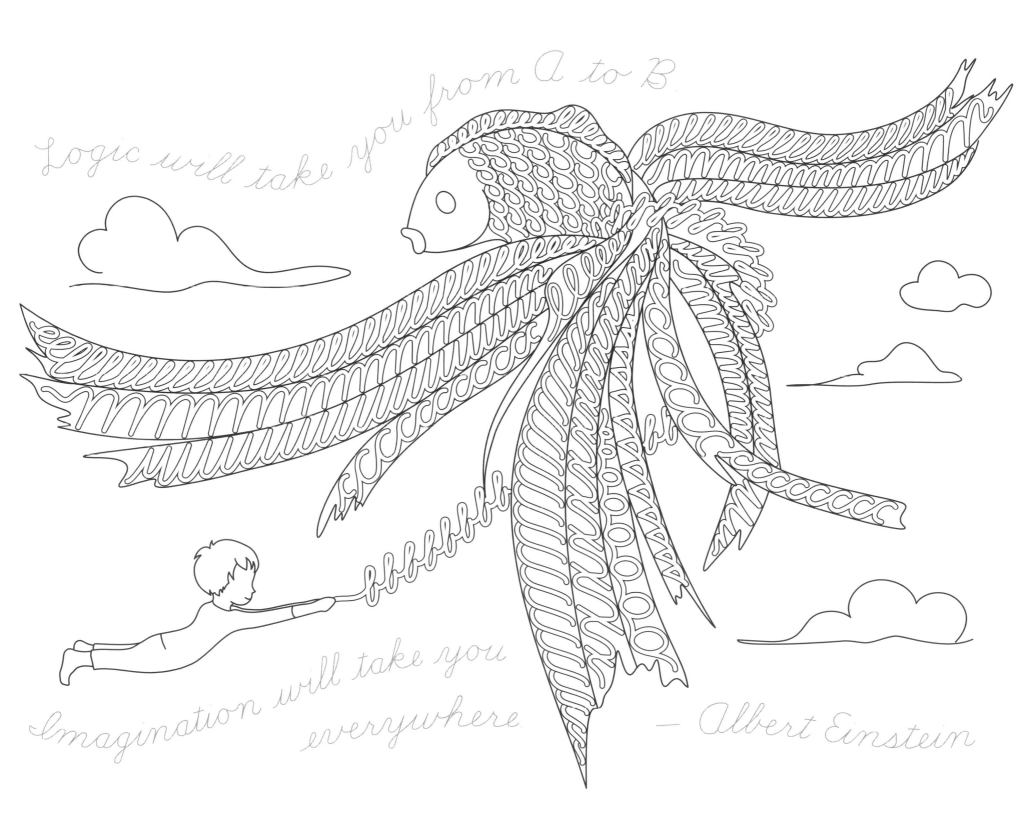

Practice

Logic will take you from A to B.

Imagination will take you everywhere.

— Albert Einstein

In the variety of its charms and the power of its spell, I know of no other place in the world which can compare with it.

—Hiram Bingham

Practice

In the variety of its charms and the power of
its spell, I know of no other place in the world
which can compare with it.

— Hiram Bingham

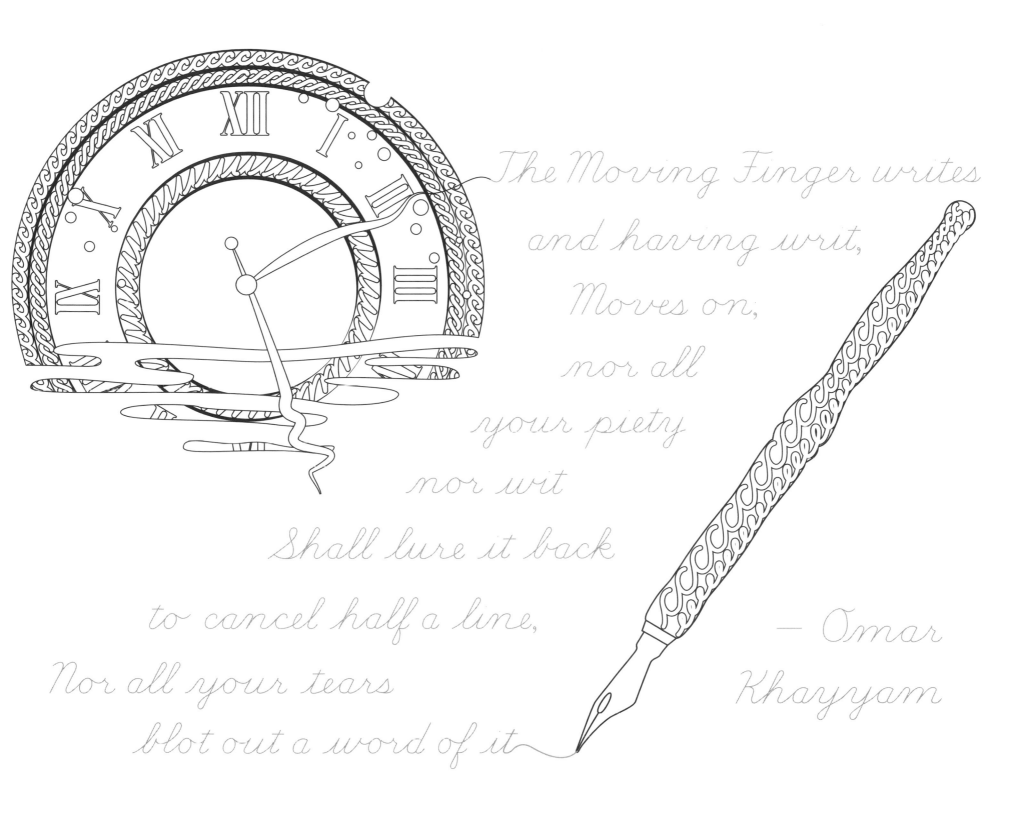

The Moving Finger writes
and having writ,
Moves on;
nor all
your piety
nor wit
Shall lure it back
to cancel half a line,
Nor all your tears
blot out a word of it

— Omar
Khayyam

Practice

The Moving Finger writes and having writ,

Moves on; nor all your piety nor wit Shall lure

it back to cancel half a line, Nor all your tears

blot out a word of it.   — Omar Khayyam

Grant that I may not
so much seek

to be consoled
to be understood,
to be loved

as to console,
as to understand,
as to love

~Saint Francis of Assisi

Practice

Grant that I may not so much seek to be
consoled as to console, to be understood as to
understand, to be loved as to love.
— Saint Francis of Assisi

Listen, lords, in bower and hall,

I sing the wonderous birth

Of brave
St. George
whose valorous arm

Rid monsters from the earth.

Practice

Listen, lords, in bower and hall,

I sing the wonderous birth

Of brave St. George whose valorous arm

Rid monsters from the earth.

Gather ye rosebuds while ye may,
Old Time is still a-flying;
And this same flower that smiles today
Tomorrow will be dying.

"To the Virgins, to Make Much of Time"
by Robert Herrick

Practice

Gather ye rosebuds while ye may, Old Time is

still a-flying; And this same flower that smiles

today, Tomorrow will be dying.

"To the Virgins, to Make Much of Time" by Robert Herrick

Either write something worth reading or do something worth writing.
— Benjamin Franklin

Keep the ink flowing

Practice

Either write something worth reading

or do something worth writing.

— Benjamin Franklin

Dum spiro, spero

While I breathe, I hope

Practice

Dum spiro, spero

While I breathe, I hope

As you grow older, you will discover that you have two hands,

one for helping yourself,

other for the helping others.

—Audrey Hepburn

Practice

As you grow older, you will discover that you

have two hands, one for helping yourself, the

other for helping others.

— Audrey Hepburn

Practice

A man may die, nations may rise and fall,

but an idea lives on.

– John F. Kennedy

We ourselves feel that what we are doing is just a

drop in the ocean

But the ocean would be less

because of that missing drop.

—Mother Teresa

Practice

We ourselves feel that what we are doing is just
a drop in the ocean. But the ocean would be less
because of that missing drop.
— Mother Teresa

Love is the only force capable of transforming an enemy into friend.

—Martin Luther King, Jr.

Practice

Love is the only force capable of transforming

an enemy into friend.

— Martin Luther King, Jr.

The kiss of the sun for pardon,

The song of the birds for mirth,

One is nearer God's Heart in a garden Than anywhere else on Earth.

"God's Garden" by Dorothy Frances Gurney

Practice

The kiss of the sun for pardon, The song of the birds for mirth, One is nearer God's heart in a garden, Than anywhere else on earth.

"God's Garden" by Dorothy Frances Gurney

WRITE

Reach high, for stars lie hidden in your soul. Dream deep, for every dream precedes the goal.

—Ralph Vaull Starr

Practice

Reach high, for stars lie hidden in your soul.

Dream deep, for every dream precedes the goal.

— Ralph Vaull Starr

If you hear a voice within you say "You cannot paint," then by all means paint, and that voice will be silenced.

Complete the sentence in cursive

—Vincent van Gogh

Practice

If you hear a voice within you say

"You cannot paint," then by all means paint,

and that voice will be silenced.

— Vincent van Gogh

Give me truths,
I am weary of the surfaces
for Blight by Ralph Waldo Emerson

Practice

Give me truths; for I am weary of the surfaces.

"Blight" by Ralph Waldo Emerson